This book is for

· · · · · · · · · · · · · · · · · · · · · · · · · · · · · ·

BORN

· · · · · · · · · · · · · · · · · · · · · · · · · · · · · ·

LOTS OF LOVE
FORVER & ALWAYS

· · · · · · · · · · · · · · · · · · · · · · · · · · · · · ·

D1472367

© Enchanted Rose